Through
these doors
walk the
Future of
Naval Aviation

Girls  are born to FLY

by BJ Lewis

Story by: BJ Lewis
Edited by: Chris Stead
Illustrations by: Ila Taylor Bologni
Published by: Sail and Soar Scribbles (SaSS)
Design: Chris Stead, Old Mate Media | www.oldmatemedia.com

Digital ISBN-13: 978-1-922740-03-8

Connect with BJ

Dedication: For my mother and spouse who have given me roots and wings. For my grandchildren, Hennessy and Riley, may you have the same, and for every child who needs to hear the message, "Yes, you can!"

Why can’t a girl be a flyer?

Soaring up higher and higher.

Up in the air,

flying somewhere,

this little girl’s dream was
on fire.

Adults kept telling her, “No!”

“The sky’s not where you should go!”

She knew she was smart,

and had the heart.

Her desire continued to grow.

Mrs. Driver
Job Chart
Librarian
Joe
Door Holder
Henny
Line Leader
Dolly
Light Inspector
Nick
Computer Helper
Riley
Messenger
Erik
Pet & Plant Caretaker
Susie
Trash Collector
Lindsay

FLY

She told her mother her dream,

not certain what that
would mean.

Her mom was a fan,

she said, “Yes, you can!”

More schooling while she
was a teen.

Graduation was thrilling
and fast.

All of her classes she passed.

She was ready to go,

time moved so slow,

it was off to flight school at last.

Through
these doors
walk the
Future of
Naval Aviation

Naval Aviation
has a place for you
The Marines are looking for a few good men.
Apply here
GEE!!
I WISH I WERE A MAN
I'd JOIN The NAVY
BE A MAN AND DO IT
UNITED STATES NAVY
RECRUITING
CHORD
$AF = qSC_P = \frac{1}{2}\rho V^2 SC_1$
$L = qSC_L = \frac{1}{2}\rho V^2 SC_L$
$D = qSC_D = \frac{1}{2}\rho V^2 SC_D$

In her group there was only
one girl.

So different it made her
mind swirl.

Still people said, “No!”

She said, “Let’s go!”

There’s no way her dream
would unfurl.

She ignored any negative talk.

This girl wanted to fly, not to walk.

She studied so hard,

always on guard.

Dreaming of eagles, sparrows and hawks.

NAVY
562
035
123
201
451
120
Aerodynamics
Navigation
MATHEMATICS
ENGINES
Weather

Learning to hover was hard!

She drifted all over the yard.

But once she knew how,

the feeling was, “Wow!”

She was sure to have good
marks on her card.

In this life, her time was finite.

She had to practice just right.

There was this one chance,

no backward glance,

and she worked with all of
her might.

WARNING
CAUTION
HELICOPTER
SIMULATOR

032

The path had some bumps and
some turns.

There were so many new things
to learn.

She touched a few clouds,

her mom was so proud,

she would fly with the wings
she had earned.

Once she had the mastery
to fly,

on her missions she never
asked why.

She saved a few lives,

and delivered supplies,

bringing help and hope from
the sky.

NAVY
03

Aviation
Non-Profit
Education
Technology
Arts
Engineering
MILITARY
Zoology
LAW

One little girl pushed open
a door.

To strive, to learn, and to yearn
for more.

She made her own choice,

and used her own voice,

chasing a dream that she
could adore.

No one should tell you what to do.

Your life is yours, it's uniquely you.

Be ready to fly,

aim super high,

and when you find what you love,
follow through.

LIVE YOUR DREAMS
BORN TO FLY
CO-PILOT

TODAY News
HELICOPTER SAVES 10
DAILY NEWS
EVACUATED AHEAD OF HURRICANE
CANADA
North America
UNITED STATES
NORTH PACIFIC OCEAN
NORTH ATLANTIC OCEAN
South America
BRAZIL
SOUTH PACIFIC OCEAN
SOUTH ATLANTIC OCEAN
Europe
North Asia
RUSSIA
Central Asia
Asia
CHINA
INDIA
Middle East
Africa
INDIAN OCEAN
Oceania
AUSTRALIA
TOWN's HERALD
SUPPLIES AIR LIFTED INTO TOWN
HELICOPTER
HELICOPTER GIRL INTERVIEW

There are so many dreams
to be had.

Doctors can cure and singers
are rad.

Make your own trail,

tell your own tale.

Find your purpose and always
be glad.

For all little girls, to your dreams take hold.

Be strong, be daring, and always be bold.

Find a dream you crave,

be nothing but brave,

and you will earn your own wings of gold.

ELEMENTARY SCHOOL

You Were Born to Fly

AMELIA EARHART

WALLY FUNK

BESSIE COLEMAN

MAE JEMISON

YOUR PHOTO HERE

MARGARET THATCHER

GRACE HOPPER

PATSY MINK

MADELEINE ALBRIGHT

EILEEN COLLINS

RUTH BADER GINSBURG

HARRIET QUIMBY

KATHERINE JOHNSON

THE END

Trailblazing Women

Madeleine Albright: Served as the first female United States Secretary of State.

Author BJ Lewis by her UH-3H helicopter in Bahrain.

Grace Hopper: Was a computer pioneer. During World War II, she was rejected because of her age and diminutive size. She persisted and received a waiver into the U.S. Naval Reserve. She retired from the Navy as a rear admiral at 79 — the oldest serving officer in the armed forces.

Wally Funk: Volunteered in 1961 for the "Women in Space" Program, submitting to rigorous physical and mental tests. Only 13 of the initial group passed the testing.

Ruth Bader Ginsburg: Was a U.S. lawyer who served as a Justice of the Supreme Court and spent her legal career as an advocate for equality and women's rights.

Bell 429 helicopter demonstration; BJ is in the red hat.

Katherine Johnson: Working in a black computing section of NASA, she calculated the path for the spaceship that put the first U.S. astronaut in space.

Margaret Thatcher: Was a British stateswoman who served as Prime Minister of the UK. She was the first woman to hold that office.

Patsy Mink: Was the first woman of color to serve in the U.S. Congress. She sponsored the Title IX law stating: "No person in the United States shall, on the basis of sex, be excluded from participation in, be denied the benefits of, or be subjected to discrimination under any education program or activity receiving Federal financial assistance."

"Do not go where the path may lead, go instead where there is no path and leave a trail." – Ralph Waldo Emerson

Huey standing by for the Space Shuttle recovery at Edwards Air Force Base.

Eileen Collins: Was the first woman to pilot and, later, to command a U.S. space shuttle.

Bessie Coleman: Was the first African American, and the first Native American, woman pilot. No U.S. flight schools would train her because she was African American and a woman. She moved to France and received her pilot's license in 1921.

Harriet Quimby: Was a pioneering pilot and the first American woman to earn a pilot's license.

Mae Jemison: Is a doctor, engineer, and astronaut. She was the first African American woman in space.

Amelia Earhart: Was an American aviation pioneer. She was the first female pilot to fly solo across the Atlantic Ocean.

BJ's first shipboard landing was on the USS Inchon. The CH-53E is one of the biggest helicopters in the world.

BJ is in the front right seat executing a rescue in a UH-1N (Huey) Helicopter.

BJ demonstrating a Bell 505 in Rio de Janeiro, Brazil.

www.ingramcontent.com/pod-product-compliance
Ingram Content Group UK Ltd.
Pitfield, Milton Keynes, MK11 3LW, UK
UKHW060119010826
14089UKWH00005B/60

9 798985 179514